Picture Dictionary

Contents

Published by Ladybird Books Ltd
A Penguin Company
Penguin Books Ltd, 80 Strand, London WC2R 0RL, UK
Penguin Books Australia Ltd, Camberwell, Victoria, Australia
Penguin Books (NZ) Ltd, 67 Apollo Drive, Rosedale, North Shore 0632, New Zealand

3 5 7 9 10 8 6 4

ISBN: 978-184646-723-3

Printed in China

Picture Dictionary

compiled by Geraldine Taylor
illustrated by Gaynor Berry

Aa

aeroplane

flying an aeroplane

animal

pet animals

acrobat

a circus acrobat

alligator

a green alligator

answer

6+4=10

the answer is ten

actor

an actor on the stage

alphabet

ABCDEFG
HIJKLMN
OPQRSTU
VWXYZ

letters of the alphabet

ant

a line of ants

address

Mr C Gull
3 Beach Road
Sandycliff

writing the address

ambulance

a hospital ambulance

apple

a shiny apple

advertisement

ZOOM

a car advertisement

anchor

a ship's anchor

apron

a clean apron

4

aquarium

fish in an aquarium

astronaut

an astronaut on the moon

baby

a baby playing

arm

a broken arm

astronomer

an astronomer
looking at stars

bag

a shopping bag

arrow

a bow and arrow

atlas

THE
LADYBIRD
PICTURE
ATLAS

a world atlas

baker

a baker making bread

artist

an artist painting

audience

a theatre audience

ball

a beach ball

asleep

asleep in bed

Bb

balloon

hot-air balloons

banana	bee	blanket
a ripe banana	bees around their nest	wrapped in a blanket
basket	bell	boat
a basket of washing	ringing a bell	a blue boat
bath	bicycle	bonfire
having a bath	riding a bicycle	a big bonfire
bear	bird	book
a polar bear	a bird with a worm	a funny book
bed	birthday	bottle
bunk beds	a birthday cake	bottles of fizzy orange

box

a cat in a box

brush

a scrubbing brush

button

coloured buttons

boy

a boy fishing

bubble

blowing bubbles

Cc

breakfast

eating breakfast

bus

a bus stop

cactus

a prickly cactus

brick

building bricks

butcher

a butcher slicing meat

cake

chocolate cake

bridge

a bridge over the river

butterfly

a pretty butterfly

calculator

a pocket calculator

calendar	**castle**	**chair**
look at the calendar	a castle and moat	a rocking chair
camera a camera and film	**cat** a ginger cat	**chimney** a chimney stack
canoe paddling a canoe	**caterpillar** a green furry caterpillar	**chimpanzee** a baby chimpanzee
car a racing car	**cave** a dark cave	**chocolate** a bar of chocolate
carpet a roll of carpet	**ceiling** a yellow ceiling	**church** going to church

city

a big city

computer

a desk-top computer

Dd

clock

a wall clock

cook

a ship's cook

dancer

a ballet dancer

cloud

dark clouds

countryside

in the countryside

day

Sunday	Monday	Tuesday	Wednesday
Thursday	Friday	Saturday	

days of the week

clown

circus clowns

crowd

a crowd of people

dentist

at the dentist's

comb

a pink comb

cup

a cup of coffee

desert

a sandy desert

desk
an office desk

different
different shoes

dog
a sleepy dog

detective
a detective looking for clues

digger
a yellow digger

doll
a rag doll

diamond
a diamond ring

dinosaur
a spiky dinosaur

door
a brown door

dice
a pair of dice

diver
a deep-sea diver

dragon
a fiery dragon

dictionary
a picture dictionary

doctor
a doctor on call

drawing
a drawing of a cat

dream

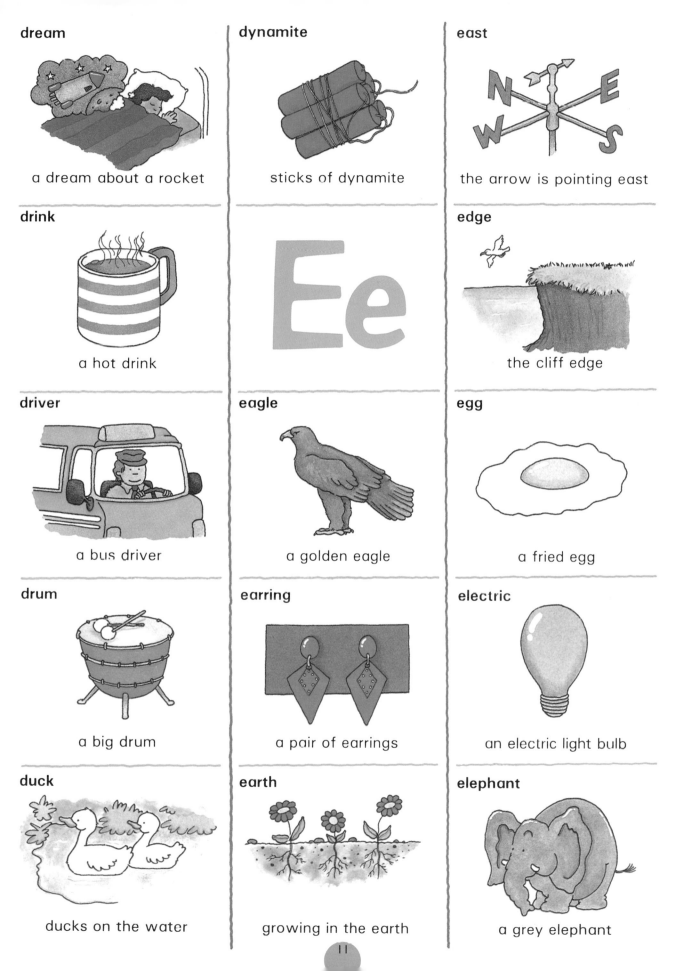

a dream about a rocket

drink

a hot drink

driver

a bus driver

drum

a big drum

duck

ducks on the water

dynamite

sticks of dynamite

Ee

eagle

a golden eagle

earring

a pair of earrings

earth

growing in the earth

east

the arrow is pointing east

edge

the cliff edge

egg

a fried egg

electric

an electric light bulb

elephant

a grey elephant

engine

checking the engine

evening

the sun sets in the evening

explosion

BANG!

a loud explosion

entrance

WAY IN ➡

go in through the entrance

exhibition

an art exhibition

Ff

envelope

a yellow envelope

exit

CLOSED

WAY OUT

go out through the exit

farm

farm animals

equipment

diving equipment

experiment

a scientific experiment

feather

a peacock's feather

escalator

UP

DOWN

a moving escalator

explorer

an explorer on safari

fence

a wooden fence

field	**flag**	**fog**
a field of wheat	a pirates' flag	thick fog
finger	**flamingo**	**footprint**
a sore finger	pink flamingos	a set of footprints
fire	**florist**	**forest**
a log fire	a florist's shop	a pine forest
fireworks	**flour**	**fork**
a fireworks display	a bag of flour	a silver fork
fish	**flower**	**fountain**
a shoal of fish	a bunch of flowers	a water fountain

friend	furniture	garden
best friends	pieces of furniture	digging the garden
frog		gate
a jumping frog	**Gg**	a wooden gate
frost	gale	ghost
frost on the window	trees blowing in a gale	a spooky ghost
fruit	game	giant
a bowl of fruit	playing a game	a happy giant
fur	garage	girl
a kitten with soft fur	a double garage	a girl skipping

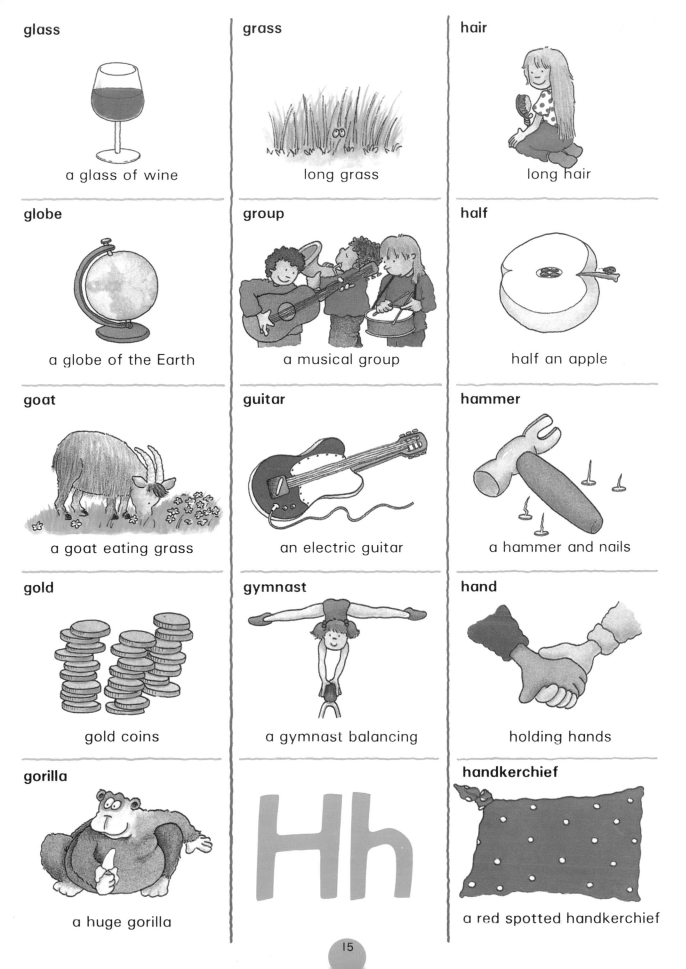

glass

a glass of wine

grass

long grass

hair

long hair

globe

a globe of the Earth

group

a musical group

half

half an apple

goat

a goat eating grass

guitar

an electric guitar

hammer

a hammer and nails

gold

gold coins

gymnast

a gymnast balancing

hand

holding hands

gorilla

a huge gorilla

Hh

handkerchief

a red spotted handkerchief

happy	hill	house
a happy face	a green hill	a pink house
hat	**hippopotamus**	**hurricane**
a top hat	a wallowing hippopotamus	a violent hurricane
heart	**hole**	**Ii**
a heart-shaped balloon	digging a hole	
helicopter	**horse**	**ice**
flying a helicopter	a rocking horse	broken ice
helmet	**hospital**	**iceberg**
a crash helmet	in hospital	a floating iceberg

ice cream	**instrument**	**jacket**
an ice cream cone	musical instruments	a checked jacket
icicle	**invitation**	**jam**
a melting icicle	a party invitation	strawberry jam
ill	**iron**	**jar**
the boy is ill	a steam iron	an empty jar
ink	**island**	**jeans**
a bottle of ink	a desert island	blue jeans
insect		**jeep**
a group of insects	Jj	an open-top jeep

jellyfish

a wobbly jellyfish

jug

a jug of milk

Kk

jewellery

a jewellery box

juggler

a skilful juggler

kaleidoscope

kaleidoscope patterns

jigsaw

a jigsaw puzzle

juice

orange juice

kangaroo

a jumping kangaroo

jockey

jockeys in a race

jump

the high jump

kettle

a boiling kettle

journey

going on a journey

jungle

in the jungle

key

a bunch of keys

18

king 	**knife**	**koala**
a king on his throne	cutting with a knife	a koala and its baby
kiss	**knight**	**Ll**
a kiss on the cheek	a knight in armour	
kitchen	**knitting**	**label**
cooking in the kitchen	knitting a jumper	a white label
kite	**knob**	**lace**
flying a kite	a red door knob	a lace tablecloth
kitten	**knot**	**ladder**
a playful kitten	tying a knot	a long ladder

ladybird

a red ladybird

lemon

a sliced lemon

lion

a roaring lion

lake

a boating lake

letter

writing a letter

loaf

loaves of bread

lamp

a table lamp

library

reading in the library

log

a log cabin

lawn

mowing the lawn

lid

a striped tin lid

luggage

a lot of luggage

leaf

a green leaf

lightning

thunder and lightning

Mm

machine

a sewing machine

match

a box of matches

milk

a carton of milk

magic

a magic carpet

medicine

a bottle of medicine

mirror

a hand mirror

magnet

a horseshoe magnet

menu

MENU

soup

fish

pizza

ice cream

fruit

look at the menu

model

a model aeroplane

man

a young man

mermaid

a beautiful mermaid

money

counting money

map

a treasure map

microwave

a microwave oven

monkey

a monkey swinging

21

moon

a crescent moon

mud

covered in mud

nature

class 3b

a nature display

morning

the sun rises in the morning

museum

visiting a museum

necklace

a ruby necklace

motorcycle

riding a motorcycle

Nn

needle

a needle and thread

mountain

snow-capped mountains

nail

a box of nails

neighbour

next-door neighbours

mouse

a mouse nibbling cheese

name

Megan   Billy

Jenny

Robert Peter

name tags

nest

a bird's nest

net

a fishing net

north

the arrow is pointing north

oak

an oak tree

newspaper

reading the newspaper

notebook

notes

a blue notebook

oar

wooden oars

night

a starry night

nurse

a hospital nurse

octopus

an octopus on a rock

nightmare

a scary nightmare

nut

a bag of nuts

office

a busy office

noise

a loud noise

Oo

oil

OIL

cans of oil

optician

at the optician's

outside

looking outside

palace

a grand palace

orange

peeling an orange

oven

a pie in the oven

panda

a black and white panda

orchard

an apple orchard

owl

a barn owl

paper

wrapping paper

ostrich

an ostrich running

Pp

parachute

a parachute jump

outline

drawing the outline

paint

a paint box

parrot

a colourful parrot

24

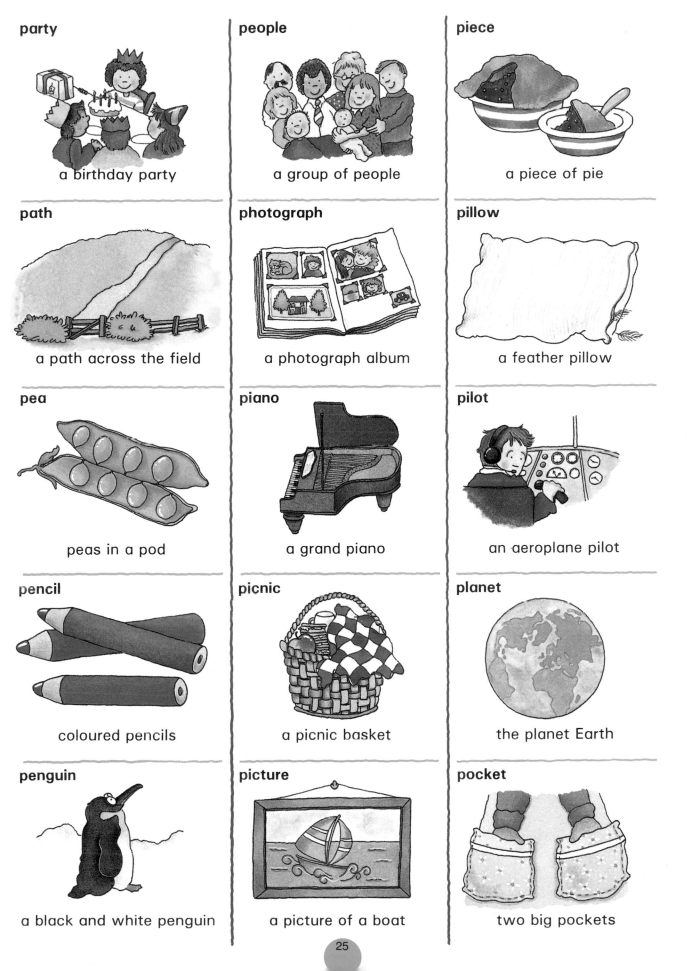

party

a birthday party

people

a group of people

piece

a piece of pie

path

a path across the field

photograph

a photograph album

pillow

a feather pillow

pea

peas in a pod

piano

a grand piano

pilot

an aeroplane pilot

pencil

coloured pencils

picnic

a picnic basket

planet

the planet Earth

penguin

a black and white penguin

picture

a picture of a boat

pocket

two big pockets

post office

at the post office

Qq

quilt

a patchwork quilt

prize

first prize

quarter

cut into quarters

quiz

BILL 56   BOB 23

a quiz show

puddle

splashing in a puddle

queen

a queen on her throne

Rr

puppet

a glove puppet

question

what's your name?

asking a question

rabbit

a pet rabbit

puppy

a hungry puppy

quiet

ssh...be quiet!

race

FINISH

a running race

radio

a portable radio

reflection

a reflection in the mirror

ring

a gold ring

railway

railway lines

refrigerator

a full refrigerator

river

a winding river

rain

rain drops

restaurant

eating in a restaurant

road

crossing the road

rainbow

colours of the rainbow

rhinoceros

a charging rhinoceros

robot

a toy robot

recipe

a recipe book

ribbon

a spotted ribbon

rock

sitting on a rock

roof

a tiled roof

Ss

scientist

a scientist at work

room

a dining room

sand

sandcastles

scissors

sharp scissors

rope

a coil of rope

sandwich

a plate of sandwiches

seashell

pretty seashells

rose

a red rose

saucepan

a saucepan of milk

shadow

a long shadow

ruler

a wooden ruler

school

learning at school

shampoo

a bottle of shampoo

28

sheep	**snail**	**soup**
a flock of sheep	a snail on a leaf	a bowl of soup
ship	**snake**	**south**
a steam ship	a slithering snake	the arrow is pointing south
shoe	**snow**	**spaceship**
a pair of shoes	playing in the snow	a model spaceship
skeleton	**soap**	**spaghetti**
a human skeleton	a bar of soap	a plate of spaghetti
sky	**somersault**	**spider**
clouds in the sky	turning a somersault	a big black spider

square	submarine	**Tt**
a blue square	a yellow submarine	
stairs	**suitcase**	**table**
coming down the stairs	an open suitcase	a round table
stamp	**sun**	**tail**
a postage stamp	hot sun	a long tail
star	**supermarket**	**telephone**
a shooting star	shopping at the supermarket	a ringing telephone
station	**swan**	**television**
a railway station	a white swan	a television set

tent

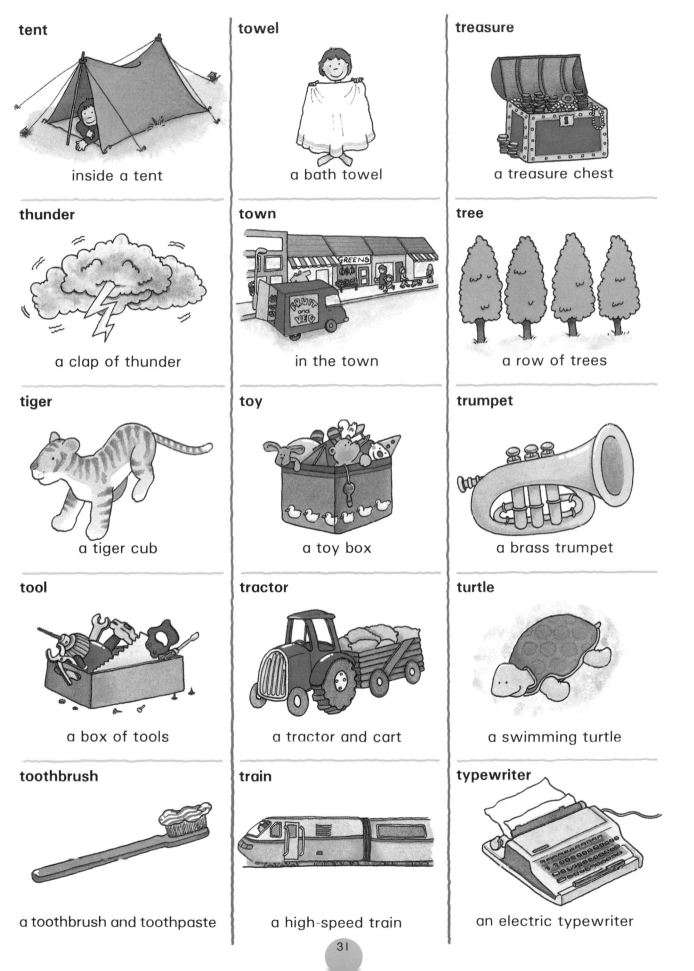

inside a tent

towel

a bath towel

treasure

a treasure chest

thunder

a clap of thunder

town

in the town

tree

a row of trees

tiger

a tiger cub

toy

a toy box

trumpet

a brass trumpet

tool

a box of tools

tractor

a tractor and cart

turtle

a swimming turtle

toothbrush

a toothbrush and toothpaste

train

a high-speed train

typewriter

an electric typewriter

Uu

uniform

a nurse's uniform

vase

a vase of flowers

ugly

an ugly mask

upside down

hanging upside down

vegetable

a box of vegetables

umbrella

an open umbrella

Vv

video

a video recorder

underground

a mole underground

vacuum cleaner

a powerful vacuum cleaner

view

a view of the sea

unicorn

a white unicorn

valley

a deep valley

village

a small village

violin

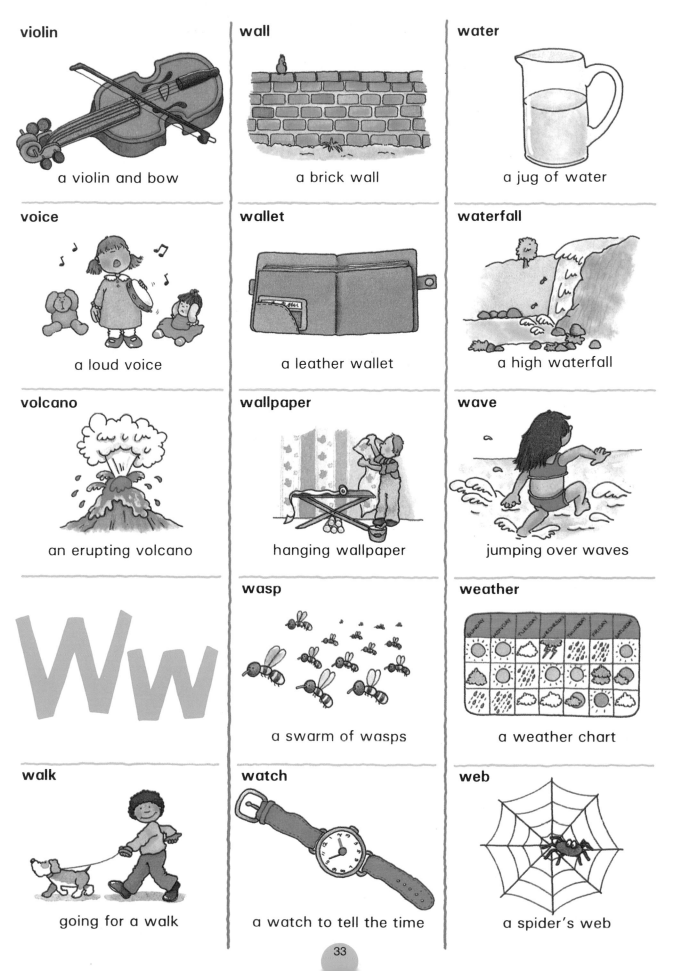

a violin and bow

wall

a brick wall

water

a jug of water

voice

a loud voice

wallet

a leather wallet

waterfall

a high waterfall

volcano

an erupting volcano

wallpaper

hanging wallpaper

wave

jumping over waves

Ww

wasp

a swarm of wasps

weather

a weather chart

walk

going for a walk

watch

a watch to tell the time

web

a spider's web

welcome

a warm welcome

whisker

six long whiskers

window

a broken window

west

the arrow is pointing west

whisper

a soft whisper

wolf

a grey wolf

whale

a blue whale

whistle

a silver whistle

woman

a woman reading

wheel

bicycle wheels

wind

blown off by the wind

world

a map of the world

wheelbarrow

a garden wheelbarrow

windmill

an old windmill

worm

a wriggly worm

X x

X-ray

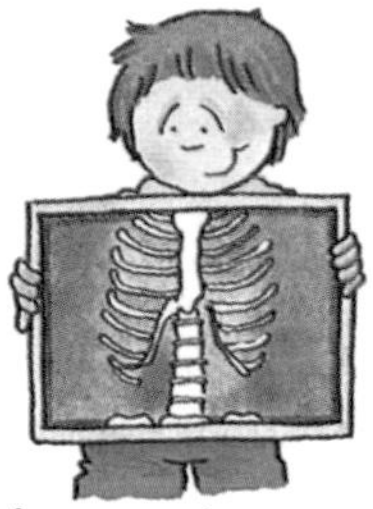

an X-ray photograph

xylophone

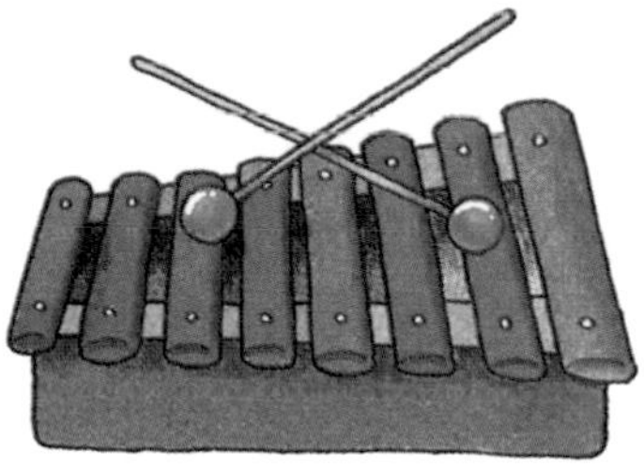

a wooden xylophone

Y y

yawn

a sleepy yawn

year

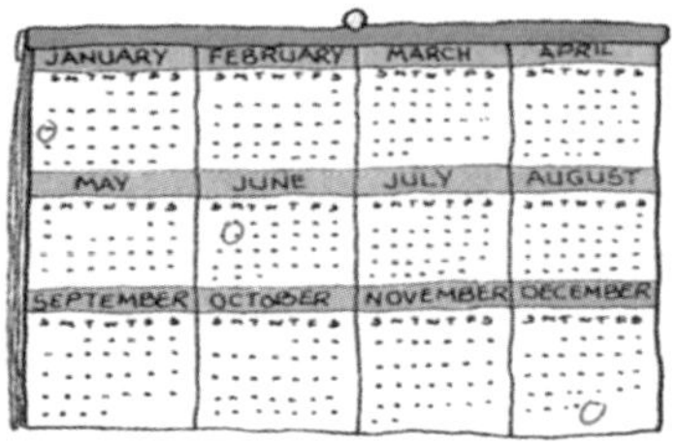

months of the year

yogurt

a pot of yogurt

yolk

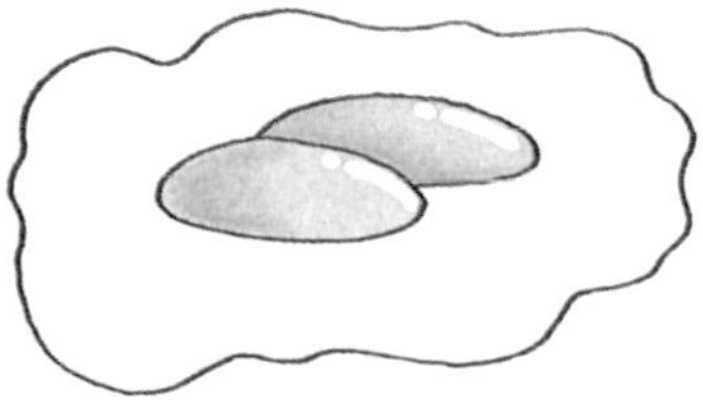

two yolks!

yak

a hairy yak

yo-yo

a red and yellow yo-yo

Z z

zebra

a striped zebra

zip

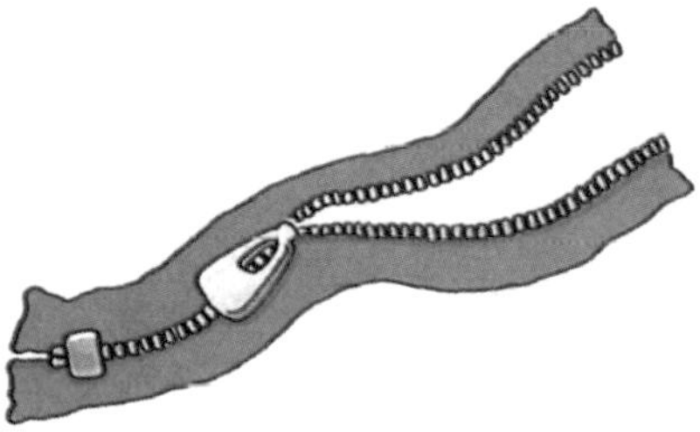

a zip fastener

zodiac

signs of the zodiac

zoo

animals in the zoo

My body

ear

eyebrow

mouth

chin

lip

neck

hair

nose

tongue

eye

teeth

cheek

Clothes

shorts

mittens

pyjamas

blouse

scarf

shirt

tie

trousers

dress

sweater/jumper

sandals

boots

slippers

36

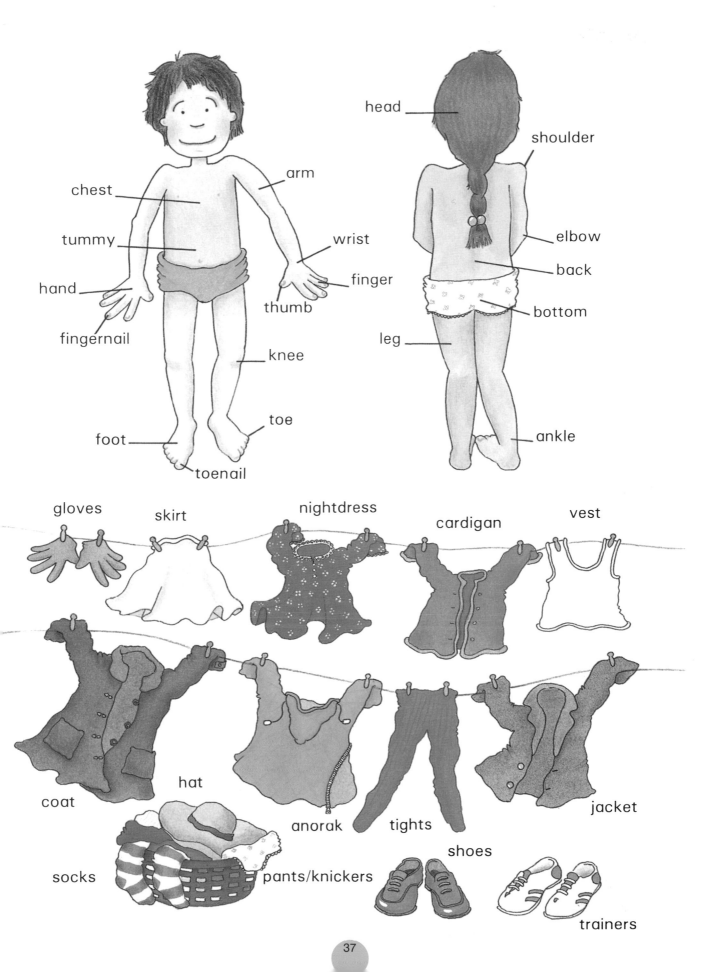

chest

arm

tummy

wrist

hand

finger

fingernail

thumb

knee

toe

foot

toenail

head

shoulder

elbow

back

bottom

leg

ankle

gloves

skirt

nightdress

cardigan

vest

coat

hat

anorak

tights

jacket

socks

pants/knickers

shoes

trainers

Families

grandad/grandpa

mother/mum

father/dad

son

granny/grandma

daughter

husband

sister   brother

wife

baby

uncle

twins

cousin

aunt

38

Food

biscuits

milk

chicken

jam

beefburger

ham

eggs

vegetables

juice

bread

salad

yogurt

sausages

sauce

cheese

meat

pizza

sugar

spaghetti

fruit

Shops

toy shop   butcher   greengrocer   florist

zero **Numbers**

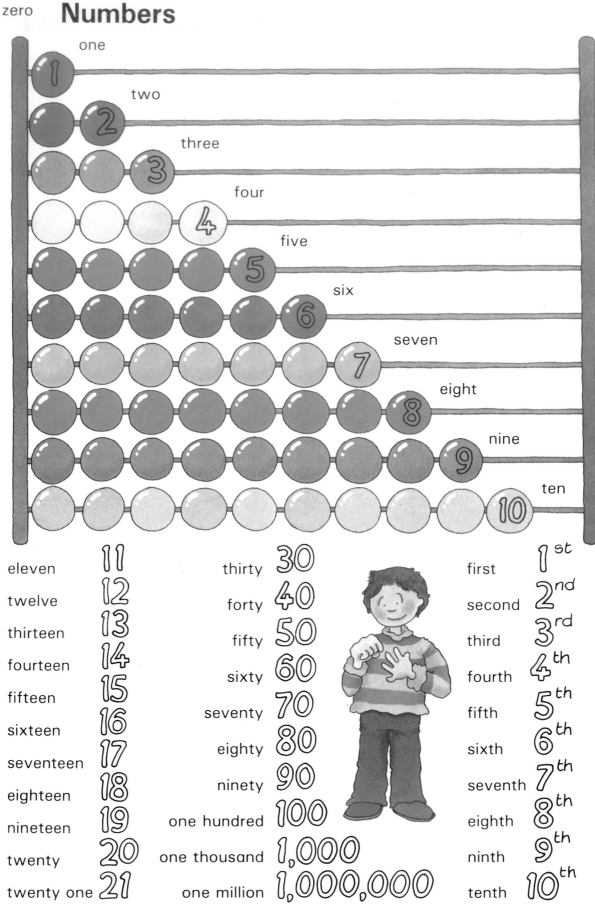

one 1
two 2
three 3
four 4
five 5
six 6
seven 7
eight 8
nine 9
ten 10

eleven 11
twelve 12
thirteen 13
fourteen 14
fifteen 15
sixteen 16
seventeen 17
eighteen 18
nineteen 19
twenty 20
twenty one 21

thirty 30
forty 40
fifty 50
sixty 60
seventy 70
eighty 80
ninety 90
one hundred 100
one thousand 1,000
one million 1,000,000

first 1st
second 2nd
third 3rd
fourth 4th
fifth 5th
sixth 6th
seventh 7th
eighth 8th
ninth 9th
tenth 10th

Days of the week

Sunday   Thursday

Monday   Friday

Tuesday   Saturday

Wednesday

Months of the year

January   July

February   August

March   September

April   October

May   November

June   December

Shapes and colours

a red rectangle

an orange star

a yellow heart

a green oval

a blue circle

a purple triangle

a pink square

a brown diamond

a black oval

a red heart

a grey rectangle

a white triangle

a turquoise diamond

a green square
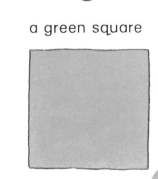

a yellow star

an orange circle
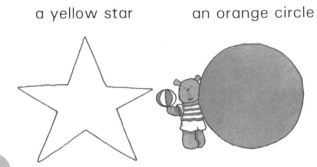

41

Doing words

read

sit

buy

sleep

dress

dry

sing

write

wash

ride

pull

push

wave

eat

jump

drink

walk

run

stop

go

talk

listen

42

Opposite words

up

down

hot

cold

tall

short

dirty

clean

old

new

empty

full

thin

fat

light

heavy

slow

on

off

fast

top

sad

happy

big

little

bottom

43

Words we write a lot

a	comes	had	made	play	up
about	coming	has	make	played	upon
after		have	me	playing	
all		having	more		
am	did	he	my		very
an	do	her	myself	said	
and	doing	here		saw	
are	down	him		see	want
as		his	new	she	was
at			nice	so	we
away	for		no	some	went
	from	I	not		were
		if			what
back		in		that	when
be	get	into	of	the	where
because	getting	is	off	their	who
but	go	it	old	them	with
	goes		on	then	
	going		only	there	
came	good	like	or	they	you
can	got	look	other	this	your
come		looking	our	to	

Spelling checklist

A

a	44	arrow	5	bed	6	brush	7
about	44	artist	5	bee	6	bubble	7
acrobat	4	as	44	beefburger	39	bus	7
actor	4	asleep	5	bell	6	but	44
address	4	astronaut	5	bicycle	6	butcher	7, 39
advertisement	4	astronomer	5	big	43	butterfly	7
aeroplane	4	at	44	bird	6	button	7
after	44	atlas	5	birthday	6	to buy	42
all	44	audience	5	biscuits	39		
alligator	4	August	41	black	41		
alphabet	4	aunt	38	blanket	6	**C**	
am	44	away	44	blouse	36	cactus	7
ambulance	4			blue	41	cake	7
an	44			boat	6	calculator	7
anchor	4	**B**		body	36-37	calendar	8
and	44	baby	5, 38	bonfire	6	came	44
animal	4	back	37, 44	book	6	camera	8
ankle	37	bag	5	boots	36	can	44
anorak	37	baker	5	bottle	6	canoe	8
answer	4	ball	5	bottom	37, 43	car	8
ant	4	balloon	5	box	7	cardigan	37
apple	4	banana	6	boy	7	carpet	8
April	41	basket	6	bread	39	castle	8
apron	4	bath	6	breakfast	7	cat	8
aquarium	5	be	44	brick	7	caterpillar	8
are	44	bear	6	bridge	7	cave	8
arm	5, 37	because	44	brother	38	ceiling	8
				brown	41	chair	8